G000141096

FOOD INNOVATIONS

AN APPROACH TO EATING ON A WHEAT, DAIRY, AND YEAST-FREE DIET

By SARAH BUN

PublishAmerica
Baltimore

First printing

ISBN: 1-4241-5828-1
PUBLISHED BY PUBLISHAMERICA, LLLP
www.publishamerica.com
Baltimore

Printed in the United States of America

DEDICATION

*This book is dedicated to my father,
the late culinary connoisseur,
who taught me everything I needed to know
about being human, eating, and cooking.*

ACKNOWLEDGEMENTS

JESUS: Without you, this book would not have been born.
KELLY, TUYEN, AND MOM: Thanks for being the taste testers of my recipes and giving me feedbacks and honest opinions on each creation.
KARINA: Thanks for your ongoing support and encouragement.
MR. & MRS. VETRANO: Who knew that after twelve years, I still remember what you have taught me. Thanks for being awesome mentors and teachers.
DR. MILLER: Thanks for cheering me on and handing me the facts.
PA TEAM: Thanks for your understanding.

Table of Contents

PART III: RESOURCES

FOREWORD

I first met Sarah Bun when she came to my clinic to receive Bowen therapy. Since I have studied herbology and nutrition, we also discussed diet, and I made some recommendations regarding supplements that would benefit her as well.

Sarah impressed me from the very beginning with her tenacity to improve her health against so many obstacles she faced. Her determination for optimal health has fed her desire to write this book and help other people toward a healthier lifestyle.

I see in Sarah a passion for helping others who are suffering with health issues similar to that which she has struggled with for so long. Sarah is full of hope and does not let go of that. She finds answers instead of giving in to her challenges.

Organized for easy use, this material makes for a very user-friendly book. Sarah apparently has spent much of her life researching and living out the information she presents here.

This book contains great tips for making diet and lifestyle changes easier, so that it is actually possible for one to make healthier choices, leading to healthier habits and, finally, a healthy lifestyle.

Brenda Briscoe
Certified Natural Health Professional
Registered Massage Therapist

INTRODUCTION

Cooking is my passion. At five, I convinced my mother to let me try at frying an egg. She hesitated, thinking that I was going to wreak havoc in the kitchen and create more mess for her to clean up. My insistence and determination had paid off. My first attempt at cooking was a success.

Throughout the years, cooking became a hobby that I practice in my spare time. I hosted dinner parties, planned events, and cooked for friends and family. Two summers ago, I coordinated and hosted a lavish Etiquettes and graduation dinner party at a restaurant for my former students and their parents. It was a night full of fun, food, and laughter. It was joyful seeing how food can spread love and bring smiles to people's faces. It brings me a sense of peace when I cook, even though the cleaning up, is not something that I look forward to. But, all is well that ends well.

Because I enjoy cooking and love food, it is easy to lose myself when I am surrounded by food. It is even easier neglecting how I feel after I eat. Food is good for us, I remind myself. I would not think that the culprit creating havoc in my body is something that Nature has provided for us, until I met a few alternative health doctors.

After explaining to them the decades of respiratory ailments, nasal congestion, allergies, and sinus troubles that I had endured, these doctors suggested that I modify my diet and minimize my intake of wheat and dairy. "This diet should not be hard," I told myself. I thought the trick was simply avoidance and elimination. I also thought that coming from a line of cooks, and my being passionate about the culinary arts, would make cooking easy for me. But, I was wrong! Little did I know that embarking on this journey meant challenging myself emotionally and physically to good length.

A CULINARY ESCAPE

Through my triumphs and frustrations and my agony and joy, I decided to share my experience with the world through a cookbook. My father, whom I called the late culinary connoisseur, had imparted in me with the belief that food is love. Food brings joy and togetherness. In sharing these recipes, I am hoping to achieve what food will bring. When you use these recipes, remember that food is not our enemy. There are ways to rise above our situation. All we need to do is look within.

Before we begin our culinary journey together, I assume that you already know much about why you want to be on this particular diet. Since there are books and resources out there that explain in depth about living on a wheat, dairy, and yeast-free diet, the conditions and the symptoms associated with the consumption of foods containing these products, this cookbook will focus mainly on the creative, spiritual, and practical aspects of this diet.

While the recipes make up the core of this book, I have included ideas to help you look at food in a creative way – to explore, experiment, and enjoy. I will explain ways on how you can be a master of your own cooking, how cooking can be fun, and frustration-free.

To make navigation through this cookbook more accessible, I have organized the book into three sections. Part I: The Innovations, briefly explains the methodology of this diet and includes a shopping list to assist in planning what to buy when making a dish. Part II: The Food, makes up the core of this cookbook. And Part III: Resources, serve as a guide.

In this cookbook, I have also decided to take my passion up to a new level by focusing and experimenting with new flavors and ingredients. The recipes contain in this book combine Eastern and Western flavors to make classic dishes that you have heard of and eaten. All dishes have been created using a blend of my own combination of spices.

I also strive to keep the ingredients short and simple. Occasionally, you will run into a few recipes that are long, but with the effort that you put in to make them, you will realize it is well worth it. In addition, the ingredients are simple enough that you can add and subtract whatever you want. I have also included tips on some recipes to coordinate a better cooking experience for you.

Throughout the book, you will notice that I have used the word sweetener in the recipes instead of sugar or oil instead of corn or canola oil. The underlying reason is that there are various types of sweeteners and oils that you can use. It is unnecessary to purchase a particular sugar or oil for use in this book. What sweeteners to use, oils to fry with, or salt to season a dish with, you already have in your home. When purchasing any ingredients, always read the labels.

It is my hope that through this cookbook, you will be empowered and will find joy in cooking. Whether you are cooking for yourself or someone in your care, allow this powerful source to transform your life. Let food give you the energy you need to live a life full of vitality, endurance, and stamina.

PART I:
THE INNOVATIONS

WHY WHEAT, DAIRY, AND YEAST-FREE?

Since our needs are complex and our body composition is different, we react to foods differently. Not everyone reacts the same way and to the same foods. Some people could react to less common food allergens such as carrots and vanilla. Others react to the most common food allergens such as milk, peanuts, shellfish, eggs, wheat, and nuts.

I chose wheat, dairy, and yeast as the basis of this cookbook and not corn and soy or nuts and shellfish, because it is a challenge creating dishes without them. After countless hours combing through aisles at specialty and grocery stores, I found, to my amazement, that almost all foods contain wheat and dairy as their bases, with yeast, used in some foods.

This explains why it is easy to get frustrated on this diet or any diet of elimination and avoidance. Subconsciously, we convince ourselves that there is nothing to eat since it seemed like *everything* is made of wheat and all the good stuff we believe we cannot have. In reality, we are surrounded by an abundant array of foods that we can have and enjoy. Our task is to look for them. They are there.

TAKING THE 'FUSS' OUT OF FRUSTRATIONS

In the beginning, adhering to a new diet will seem more like a burden than a blessing. The rigidity, frustration, and the mental effort required outweigh the benefits. That is what our mind and body try to convince us. Sticking to the plan requires commitment and discipline. On the one hand, abandoning the diet and going back to the old ways and habits serve as a quick escape. Going back to the way we used to eat is easier than staying on a plan that we did not plan to be on in the first place. Even if we are cooking for someone, this can be a frustrating experience for ourselves and for the other person.

I remember I stopped cooking for a season, turning the reins over to my family members. This alleviated much of the stress and tension, but it was challenging for them as well. When it was pasta night, mom cooked two kinds of pasta, regular wheat and rice. When it was roast beef sandwich night, I ate the beef and passed on the bread.

When my family members cooked for me, I also often get asked what I could and could not eat. This is because only I know my body and how it feels. Sometimes, I had no choice, but to eat what was set in front of me.

As for caring for someone like young children, they may not be at an age to be interested in reading labels, pay particular attention to every single ingredient, or know what is good for them. This is where the adults, guardians, siblings, friends, and parents come in to decide for them. This can be frustrating at times because there is only so much we can do.

One of the ways we can take the "fuss" out of our frustrations is to be open-minded. This happens when we allow our mind to soar and run wild with food and allow it to take us to a new level of possibility thinking and higher horizons.

Another way is to keep things short and simple. This is one of the reasons why I strive to use fresh ingredients. It is easier to work with. To save time, energy, and money, buying foods that come in a canned is perfectly fine as it is a practical thing to do. The key is to do what is comfortable for you and do the best that you can in your given situation and circumstances.

Keep enough foods around the house so that you or someone in your care can safely have is another way to ease the frustration. Non-perishable items are the best. This keeps us grounded in staying committed to a diet we are supposed to stay on whether it is for a health condition or a weight loss reason. It works because when we have snacks readily available, we stick to the plan. Realistically, it is understandable if we do not. We are only human.

Being on a wheat, dairy, or yeast-free diet is a choice, a decision, and a life style difference. Even if we are advised to choose this diet for a medical condition, it is ultimately a decision and a choice we make for ourselves. This diet is no different than other diets. Accepting this diet as part of our life and not independent of ourselves is important to achieve positivity, self-acceptance, and gratitude for all that we do have.

With these ideas, it is simple to implement them in our daily routine. It requires little of us, but they can work wonders for us in the long run. One of the most important things to remember is to create this experience as normal as you can, for you and someone in your care.

In the proceeding pages, you will find a list of kitchen aids and a grocery list items. If you are ready to move on from this page, let us go.

THE ESSENTIALS:
BEFORE YOU BEGIN

Now that you are almost ready to begin cooking, a good cooking experience requires help. A good kitchen helper, such as a food processor, can opener, or rice cooker, can simplify your life. It is unnecessary to purchase the following to have a good cooking experience, you might have some or all of them already in your kitchen.

Portable indoor grill
Rice cooker
Food processor
Can opener
Spiral slicer
Crock pot
Blender
Skillet or wok
Pots
Pans
Peeler

GROCERY LIST:
ITEMS NEEDED TO CREATE DISHES IN THIS COOKBOOK

A quick and easy reference for your shopping needs.

VEGETABLES

American broccoli
Cucumber
Bean sprouts
Parsley
Cilantro
Celery
Cabbage
Edamame
Green bell pepper
Yellow bell pepper
Red bell pepper
Roma tomatoes
Yellow Squash
Yukon gold potatoes
Red potatoes
Asparagus
Purple Cabbage
Lotus root
Water chestnuts
Napa cabbage
Carrots
Kale
Baby spinach
Spinach
Fuzzy squash
Preserved cabbage
Romaine lettuce
Mixed greens

Avocado
Kelp
Peas
Black olives
Purple Yam
Yucca
Taro
Sweet potato

POULTRY

Chicken
Chicken wings
Chicken drumsticks
Chicken breasts
Cornish hen

HERBS & SPICES

Sweet Thai Basil
Oregano
Paprika
Cayenne pepper
Ginger
Ginger Powder
Garlic
Garlic Powder
Cumin
Ground coriander
Salt
Pepper
White pepper
Cinnamon
Turmeric
Dried chili pepper

FISH

Tilapia
Tuna
Salmon
Mahi-Mahi
Cod fillet
Sardines
Sea bass
Halibut

MEAT

Beef sirloin
Pork Spareribs

BIRD

Turkey
Quail

SEAFOOD

Shrimp
Crab
Scallop
Crab

GRAINS

Jasmine rice
Brown rice
Arborio rice
Brown basmati rice
White basmati rice
Corn

OIL

Olive oil
Sesame seed oil

BEANS & LEGUMES

Lentils
Garbanzo beans
Black beans
Tofu (soft, medium, firm, extra firm)
Bean curd

NUTS & SEEDS

Cashews
Pecan
Pine nuts
Peanuts
Walnuts
Almonds
Slivered almonds
Sesame Seed
Ground Flaxseed
Whole Flaxseed
Sesame tahini
Sunflower seeds

FRUITS & TROPICAL FRUITS

Granny Smith green apples
Blueberries
Strawberries
Raspberry
Honey dew melons

Pears
Kiwi
Pineapple
Jackfruit
Longan
Lychee
Papaya
Banana
Lemon
Limes
Raisins
Orange
Watermelon
Mandarin orange
Clementines
Red jujube dates
Plantain bananas

NONDAIRY

Almond milk
Soy milk
Rice ice cream

NATURAL SWEETENERS

Agave nectar
Stevia
Honey
Date sugar

MISCELLANEOUS ITEMS

Spring roll rice wrapper (found in Asian supermarkets)
Glass noodles
Rice vermicelli

Spinach spaghetti
Noodles
Green tea
Umeboshi plum paste
Fish sauce
Tamarind
Bragg's Liquid Aminos
Bragg's Raw Apple Cider Vinegar
Dry mustard
Dried shrimp
Chicken broth
Tapioca starch
Apricot preserves
Skewers
Black rice
White rice flour
Brown rice flour
Toothpicks

PART II:
THE FOOD

EXPLORE NEW POSSIBILITIES
WITH FOODS

Artists create. Whether it is a piece of painting, sculpture, or artwork, it is the artists' masterpiece. When you explore and experiment with food, you create too. You become an artist. You are an artist. The food you create becomes an idea in your mind. This idea translates and transforms onto a plate. Any dish you make becomes your masterpiece.

Explore. Exploring new possibilities with food on a wheat, dairy, and yeast-free diet gives us choices that we are unaware that we have. We need choices. We have them when we think beyond what we 'can't' have.

Habit. Make it a habit to pick out one new item each time you shop that you have not tried. Experiment with the new item in your kitchen. If you have young children, this would be a good quality time spent together and a fun way to introduce them to new foods, words, and experiences.

Fun. Cooking is fun. Trying new foods is fun too. The fun lies in how much you can do, within your power, to transform one vegetable and one meat into a different dish each time.

Flexibility. Being flexible allows us to ease our frustrations when circumstances happen beyond our control. There are days where things go awry. Things did not go as planned or anticipated. Food turned out to be disastrous even after following a recipe. When practicing being flexible, we see things we do not see. It is okay that food turns out the way it did. It can be for the better.

Freedom. You have total freedom when you are the master of your kitchen. You are in control. You can create anything you like and to your liking. The key is knowing how to exercise this freedom. If you want to use a different vinegar, sweetener, oil, salt, noodles, vegetables, meat, and seafood, that is fine. There is no rule or law that says we have to strictly follow a recipe.

Openness. As you begin to cook, invite a friend or two over to share in the joy of cooking or get the whole family to assist if possible. I like cooking with a few people because then, cooking becomes play and not work. We may even learn something new when we open our lives to others.

Love. While you are at it, put in a touch of love. We achieve better results when we put love into whatever we do. It does not even have to be a lot. A little bit goes a long way. From my experience, food comes out tastier and better even on days I experienced a 'cooker's block.' Like writer's block, there are occasions where I run out of ideas on what to make or cannot seem to express my creativity through foods. Put a little love and flavor into your food. Add a touch of "you" in there. Create your own magic in the kitchen.

Chance. Cooking is also about taking chances. On days when my creativity is at its peak, I chance upon my best creations. When I do not plan what to make, been too busy to go to the store, or miss one ingredient to make a certain dish, I invade the fridge and pantry. I grab a few items I have and throw them together to create a dish. If you have ever watched Iron Chef on the Food Network, it is the same thing except, we are not competing with anyone, but challenging ourselves to be better at what we do. You might even surprise yourself with your creation.

Master. The more you cook and practice this art, you will get better at it. If we see cooking as a task or a chore, then it will be one in our mind. When you master your own cooking, it becomes a part of you, and the more you know about it, the more you can do for others and for yourself. Only you know what is best for you.

If you are ready to cook, let us begin.

SALAD SENSATION

"To remember a successful salad is generally to remember a successful dinner; at all events, the perfect dinner necessarily includes the perfect salad."
George Ellwanger (1848-1906)
Pleasures of the Table (1902)

George Ellwanger says it well about salad even though it was quite a long time ago. The salad recipes you will find here balances out different flavors. The wonderful thing about a salad dish is that there are many possibilities and ways we can have this course with our meals. Maybe one day you feel like having a fruit salad, or a side salad, perhaps, even a salad as an entrée. Either meal, salad makes it for us in taste and flavor through our choice of meats, vegetables, fruits, and salad dressings. Speaking about salad dressings, feel free to use your favorite as well.

Now Serving...

Almond Toasted Grilled Chicken Salad
Papaya Salad in Purple Cabbage Bowl
Green Mango Salad
Spring Mix Shrimp Salad
Apple Water Chestnut Salad
Summer Punch Salad

Almond Toasted Grilled Chicken Salad

This salad uses toasted slivered almonds instead of crispy noodles.

Prep time: 15 minutes
Cook time: 15 minutes
Yields: 4

1-2 chicken breasts
Salt and black pepper
1 orange, two mandarin oranges, or 3 clementines, cut into wedges
4 cups baby spinach and mixed greens of choice
¼ cup toasted slivered almonds
¼ teaspoon toasted sesame seeds
¼ cup un-sulphured dried cranberries (optional)
Sesame Citrus Dressing

Need: portable indoor grill, pan, large salad bowl

Before grilling chicken breast, season it with salt and pepper. When done, cut chicken breasts into ¼ inch thick strips. Peel and cut citrus fruits of choice into wedges. In a shallow pan, toast almonds and sesame seeds together over medium heat until lightly brown. In a large salad bowl, add spinach, mixed greens, citrus fruit, chicken, and cranberries. Top with sesame seeds and almond. Pour Sesame Citrus dressing over.

TIP: If you like your greens to be crisp, baby spinach and mixed greens can be washed and dry in the fridge ahead of time.

Sesame Citrus Dressing

This is a sweet and tangy dressing.

Prep time: less than 5 minutes
Yields: ½ cup salad dressing

¼ cup extra virgin olive oil
½ cup of orange juice
1/8 teaspoon of sesame oil
1/8 teaspoon of dry mustard
1/8 teaspoon of agave nectar
¼ - ½ teaspoon of sesame tahini (optional)
Juice of half a lime
Salt and black pepper

Need: a small container with lid

Add all ingredients to a small container with lid. Shake. Refrigerate until ready to use.

Papaya Salad in Purple Cabbage Bowl

Try this beautiful colored salad with beef skewers.
Papaya salad makes a nice side salad or as an entrée.

Prep time: 15 minutes
Cook time: 1 minute
Stand & Chill time: 15 minutes +
Yields: 4

Citrus Basil Dressing (recipe follows)
6 cups of green unripe papaya finely shredded
1 teaspoon salt
2/3 cup of cooked shredded chicken
½ cup of cooked shrimp, shelled, de-veined, and halved
2 Roma tomatoes cut into wedges
4 purple cabbage leaves

Need: pot and large salad bowl

Prepare the dressing ahead of time. Next, soak papaya in salt water for 5 minutes. Drain and set aside to dry. In a pot, cook chicken drumsticks until well done. When done, remove and shred chicken meat. While the chicken cooks, boil shrimp. When done, shell, de-vein, and slice the shrimp in half. Cut tomatoes and de-seed. In a large salad bowl, add chicken, shrimp, and tomatoes to papaya. Add Citrus Basil dressing and mix well. Let the salad stand for 15 minutes. For an enhanced flavor, let the papaya marinate in dressing longer. Refrigerate for better results. When ready to serve, fill each purple cabbage with papaya salad.

TIP: Peeled unripe papaya reveals a soft white green color. Pre-shredded papayas are found in most Asian supermarkets. Some stores may carry whole unripe papaya, which you can shred yourself using a shredder or spiral slicer.

Citrus Basil Dressing

Prep time: 10 minutes
Yields: ¾ cup

¼ cup lime juice
¼ cup of fish sauce
¼ cup of water
2 cloves of garlic, smashed
2-3 Thai bird chili, chopped and de-seeded
2 basil, cut into ribbons
1 mint shredded
1-2 tablespoon sweetener
Roasted chopped peanuts or cashews (optional)

Need: blender or food processor

Blend or process everything together except the roasted peanuts or cashews. Refrigerate until ready to use. When ready to use, top sauce with choice of nuts. The nuts give the sauce an extra kick.

TIP: Most Asian, Latin, and American supermarkets carry fish sauce. When purchasing any product, it is idealistic to find a top quality brand of fish sauce. Always read the label for ingredients. Some contain wheat.

If you prefer, tamarind paste may be used as a substitute for fish sauce.

Green Mango Salad

This salad goes well with many dishes.
Try it as a side to an entrée or with beef skewers.

Prep time: 20 minutes
Yields: 2

1/8 cup ground, dried shrimp
2 green unripe mangos, finely shredded or cubed
¼ cup pineapple, chopped
½ teaspoon of basil, cut into ribbons
Saucy Mango Dressing (recipe follows)

Need: blender or food Processor and salad bowl

Grind the dried shrimp in a blender or food processor and set aside. In a salad bowl, add peeled and shredded mangoes and pineapple. Top with basil. Add mango dressing and mix well.

TIP: Most green mangoes are hard and sweet, but not all green mangoes are the same. The juice from the pineapple in this dish will ripen the unsweetened mango and give this fruit a nice sweet taste. The longer the mango salad sits in the juice, the riper it will get. To achieve desired sweet and tartness, your favorite sweetener may be used. Be sure not to over-dress the mango salad. You want a dry salad.

Saucy Mango Dressing

This subtle blend of sweet and sour from the pineapple and mango blends nicely together with unripe mangoes.

Prep time: 5 minutes

½ cup pineapple juice
1/8 teaspoon chili powder
2 Thai bird chili, deseeded and sliced
1 teaspoon agave nectar (optional)

Need: a small bowl

Mix everything together.

Spring Mix Shrimp Salad

A taste of Spring where the grass is green, the birds are chirping, and the sky is a clear blue. A light salad like this one will brighten up your day.

Prep time: 10 minutes
Yields: 4

1 bag of Spring mix salad or mixed greens of choice
½ cup of cooked shrimp, peeled, de-veined, halved
1/8 cup cucumber, thinly sliced
1/8 cup red onion, thinly sliced
1/16 cup rice vinegar
½ tablespoon lemon juice
½ cup olive oil
Black pepper, salt, and a pinch of sweetener as needed

Need: Spiral slicer and large salad bowl

Wash greens and let dry. Using a spiral slicer, slice cucumbers and red onion. Soak cucumbers and red onions in rice vinegar, the same kind of vinegar used on sushi rice. In a large salad bowl, add greens, cucumbers, and red onion. Add remaining liquid ingredients to salad. Stir well.

Apple Water Chestnut Salad

A nice way to start your day with a tangy and sweet salad.

Prep time: 20 minutes
Yields: 2

Plum Lime Sauce (recipe follows)
1 green Granny Smith apple, shredded
½ cup water chestnuts, shredded
1/8 cup dried un-sulphured cranberries

Need: peeler and bowl

Prepare Plum Lime Sauce ahead of time to retard the discoloration of the fruits. Next, peel and chop apples and water chestnuts to resemble thin shoestring potatoes. In a bowl, mix apples, water chestnuts, and cranberries together. Mix in Plum Lime Sauce.

Plum Lime Sauce

Prep time: 2 minutes

1 teaspoon umeboshi plum paste
1 teaspoon agave nectar
1 teaspoon of water
Juice of half a lime

Need: a small mixing bowl

Mix all the ingredients together.

TIP: Information on umeboshi is available online. Umeboshi plum and paste are found in health food stores and selected supermarkets.

Summer Punch Salad

Raw cabbage and cucumber are good for us.
They provide a soothing and refreshing treat all year round.

Prep time: 15 minutes
Marinate time: 30-1 hour
Yields: 2-4

2 cups chicken thighs or drumsticks, cooked and shredded
2 cups cucumbers, chopped
2 cups cabbage, finely shredded
2 teaspoons cilantro, chopped
2 teaspoons mint, chopped
½ cup roasted cashews, chopped (optional)
Citrus Mint Dressing (recipe follows)

Need: large pot, peeler, pan

Prepare two cups of cooked shredded chicken and set aside. Peel cucumber, slice into rounds, then cut into fours. Shred cabbage. Cut cilantro and mint. Combine all ingredients into a large pot. In a pan, roast and chop cashews, set aside. Prepare Citrus Mint Dressing. Pour sauce over salad and let stand in the fridge for 30 minutes to one hour. The longer it sits, the tastier the salad gets. Sprinkle chopped cashews when you are ready to serve.

Citrus Mint Dressing

This is the same sauce as the Citrus Basil Dressing found in this section. The difference is this sauce replaces basil with mint.

Prep time: 5 minutes
Yields: 4

¼ cup lime juice
¼ cup of fish sauce
¼ cup of water
2 cloves of garlic, smashed
2-3 Thai bird chili, chopped and de-seeded
1 - 2 tablespoons agave nectar
¼ cup roasted cashews or peanuts, chopped
2 tablespoons of cilantro, chopped

Need: small mixing bowl

In a small mixing bowl, combine all liquid ingredients together. Chop cashews or peanuts and cilantro. Add to the sauce. Mix well.

SOUPS GALORE

Soups are soothing and comforting to drink. The soups here are simple. The ingredients used are few. Because they are simple, it opens rooms for addition of vegetables and meats of your choice.

Now Serving...

Kale & Pine Nut Soup
Lotus Root & Lentil Soup
Sweet & Sour Chicken Soup
Watercress Soup
Clear Ginger Broth
Chicken with Rice & Garlic Soup
Seafood Pasta Shell Soup

Kale & Pine Nut Soup

*The roasted taste of kale gives this vitamin rich soup
its wonderful flavor.*

Prep time: 5 minute
Cook time: 25 minutes
Yields: 4

1 ½ - 2 cups kale, chopped to bite-size pieces
½ tablespoon Bragg's Raw Apple Cider Vinegar
½ tablespoon olive oil
½ teaspoon salt
½ teaspoon black pepper
4 cups chicken broth
½ cup water
½ cup pine nuts

Need: pot and oven

Season kale with apple cider vinegar, olive oil, salt, and pepper. Bake uncovered in the oven for 10-15 minutes at 400 degrees. While the kale bakes, move on to work on the soup base.

Bring chicken broth and water to a boil. Add pine nut to soup. Remove from heat and add kale.

TIP: Kale covered in foil locks in the moisture to give kale a softer texture. Bragg's Raw Apple Cider Vinegar is found in health food stores. When using canned chicken broth, read the label. Some contain yeast.

Lotus Root Soup with Lentils

This is another hearty soup loaded with nutritional benefits.

Prep time: 15 minutes
Cook time: 1 hr - to 6 hours
Yields: 4

2 segments of lotus root, sliced
1½ slab spare ribs, cut
½ cup lentils
8-10 cups water
2 red dates
Season with salt to your taste

Need: crock pot

Wash and peel lotus roots. Slice lotus roots diagonally into slices about 1/8 inch thick. Cut spareribs into pieces. Wash lentils and add all ingredients together. Cook overnight.

TIP: Soup is thicker using a slower cooker than stove top. For a refreshing clear broth, use the stove top version. If you like the thicker soup, use a crock pot and add about ½ cup more of lentils. If you want a clear light soup, use less lentils.

Sweet & Sour Chicken Soup

No matter where you are, you have heard the benefit of drinking chicken soup. This soup is not your typical chicken soup.

Prep time: 15 minutes
Cook time: 15 - 20 minutes.
Yields: 4

2 cups of chicken with bone in, chopped
4 ½ cups broth
1/8 – ¼ teaspoon ground red chili pepper flakes
1 tablespoon green onions, finely chopped
1 tablespoon of fish sauce
Juice of half a lime
Garlic oil

Need: pot

Boil chicken in broth. When chicken is almost done, add fish sauce and bring to a boil. When done, transfer to a soup bowl. Top with green onions and garlic oil. Squeeze lime juice until desired sourness is reached. Add red chili pepper flakes and garlic oil. Stir well.

TIP: Garlic oil can be prepared by heating up a skillet in olive oil and 2 garlic cloves minced. Cook garlic until it becomes brown and crispy.

If you are using broth, make sure the soup has enough seasoning for your taste. If you feel the broth does not need additional salt, omit the fish sauce.

Watercress Soup

Some soups are good thick, but this one is good as it is, simple and light.

Prep time: 5 minutes
Cook time: 10-15 minutes
Yields: 1

1 serving of watercress
1 ½ cup of your favorite broth

Need: pot

Bring broth to a boil. Add watercress and turn off heat. Serve immediately.

Clear Ginger Broth

A soup to drink on a rainy day.

Prep time: 5 minutes
Cook time: 5 minutes
Yields: 1

1½ cups of your favorite broth
3 slices of ginger
Salt (optional)
A dash of black pepper for extra spiciness

Need: pot

Peel and cut ginger. In a pot, add broth and ginger. Bring to a boil.
Serve immediately. If desired, add more ginger.

Chicken with Rice & Garlic Soup

Here is another one of those classic soup we have all heard about.

Prep time: 15-20 minutes
Cook time: varies
Yields: 4

6 cups of broth
5 chicken wings
2 cups chicken breast, cubed
¼ cup carrot, diced
¼ cup celery, diced
¼ cup onion, diced
5 garlic cloves, smashed
½ cup brown rice
Salt and black pepper to taste
1 teaspoon of tapioca starch (optional)
Parsley for garnish

Need: crock pot

In a crock pot, add all ingredients. Let it slowly cook for at least six hours or overnight. Season with salt and pepper to taste. Garnish with a pinch of fresh or dried parsley.

Seafood Pasta Shell Soup

Pasta in soup for a change.

Prep time: 15 minutes
Cook time: 30 minutes
Servings: 4

1 cup of pasta shells
4 canned of broth
1 cup of water (optional)
1 cup shrimp, shelled with tail on
1 cup mixed seafood
1/2 cup green onions, finely chopped
¼ cup prepared garlic oil
A dash of black pepper
A dash of your favorite chili (optional)
1 teaspoon of Tianjin preserved vegetables (optional)

Need: two large pots

In one pot, prepare pasta shells according to package directions. In a separate pot, add broth and water. Bring to a boil and then simmer on very low heat. Add seafood and shrimp. When the pasta shells are ready, remove and rinse in cold water. Add to the large pot of soup. Stir. Top with green onions, garlic oil, black pepper, chili, and Tianjin preserved vegetables.

TIP: If the soup is too thick, add more broth. Tianjin preserved vegetable is made of cabbage, garlic, and salt. It is commonly added to soups to season and to bring out more flavors. This preserved vegetable can be found in Asian supermarkets.

SIZZLING STARTERS

A way to kick up the taste buds, start with a dish from Sizzling Starters. This section gets its name because some of the recipes call for spiciness. Spiciness is an option and may be omitted. You can still make a dish without the chili. Share these appetizers with friends, eat them as snacks, or as a main course dish.

Now Serving...

Edamame
Grilled Pineapple Kabobs
Lemon Garlic Shrimp with Avocado & Asparagus
Spicy Cold Tofu
Shrimp with Soy Chili Sauce
Napa Cabbage Roll
Stuffed Fuzzy Squash
Fish Ceviche over Fried Bean Curd
The Other Chips & Dips

Edamame

Edamame is a soybean pod. This quick and simple dish can be served with any main course, eaten as a breakfast meal, or munched on while hanging out with friends.

Prep time: 15 minutes
Yields: 2-4

2 cups edamame pods, cooked and shelled
½ teaspoon of Bragg's Liquid Aminos or ½ teaspoon of salt
1 teaspoon sesame oil
A pinch of cayenne
A pinch of paprika

Need: a small mixing bowl

Shell edamame pods or buy the ones already shelled. Lightly season and toss. You may add your favorite salad dressing to this or eaten plain without the spice.

Grilled Pineapple Kabobs

A simple tropical delight treat.
This goes well with a plate of white rice or Chicken Flavored Rice.

Prep time: 25-30 minutes
Cook time: 10-15
Yields: varies

½ lb – 1 lb beef sirloin or your favorite beef, thinly sliced
A few splashes of Bragg's Liquid Aminos
2-5 garlic cloves, finely chopped
½ - 1 cup of pineapple juice
Generous amount of ground black pepper
1 bunch of skewers
1-2 cups of fresh or canned pineapples, chunks

Need: charcoal or indoor portable grill

Season thinly sliced beef in Bragg's Liquid Aminos, garlic, pineapple juice, and ground black pepper. Soak skewers in water. Alternate between pineapple and beef. Grill on charcoal or portable grill.

TIP: Thinly sliced beef can be marinated quickly and does not need to stand overnight to absorb in the marinade. Beef soak in marinade can be refrigerated overnight for a more enhanced flavor. This appetizer is very versatile. You can eyeball all the ingredients, add your own spices, and vegetables.

Lemon Garlic Shrimp with Avocado & Asparagus

Attention seafood lover! This one is for you.

Prep time: 10 minutes
Cook time: 5 minutes
Yields: 4

10 shrimp, shelled, de-veined, and chopped
10 baby scallops, chopped
Salt and black pepper to taste
A pinch of cayenne pepper
1 garlic clove, minced
1 tablespoon olive oil
2 avocados halves, pit removed
Juice of half a lemon
2 blanched asparagus spears for garnish

Need: skillet and pan

Prepare shrimp. Season shrimp and scallop with salt, cayenne, and black pepper. In a pan, swirl oil around over medium to high heat. Add garlic. Stir. Cook shrimp and scallop. Add lemon juice. Stir and remove from heat. Next, slice avocado in half. Scoop out the avocado on mix it with the shrimp and scallop using the same pan. Mash lightly. Scoop mixture back into the avocado shell and eat straight from the shell. Add more lemon if desired. Garnish with a few asparagus spears on each avocado.

Spicy Cold Tofu

A refreshing alternative to an egg dish,
and you still get the protein you need.

Prep time: 10 minutes
Yields: 1-2

1 teaspoon sesame seed, toasted
1 habanero or Thai bird chili, sliced and de-seeded
1 12-16 ounces silken tofu
2 tablespoons Bragg's Liquid Aminos
1 teaspoon green onions, chopped
A splash of sesame oil (not too much, can be overpowering)
A splash of cayenne pepper

Need: shallow pan

Toast sesame seeds until lightly brown. Remove from heat and set aside. Prepare habanero or Thai bird chili and set aside. Pour silken tofu onto a plate. Top tofu with sesame seeds, chili, Bragg's Liquid Aminos, green onions, and sesame oil. Immediately serve or chill until ready to eat.

TIP: There are many varieties of tofu to choose from. Which brands to purchase depends on your taste and preference. Stores sell tofu that comes in a box that does not need to be refrigerated until opened. If you buy this one, you can prepare this dish ahead of time by chilling it in the refrigerator prior to use. Doing this, omits one step, which is chilling the tofu after you season it. This will save you time.

Shrimp with Soy Chili Sauce

This is an alternative version to shrimp with cocktail sauce.

Prep time: 15 minutes
Cooking time: 1 minutes
Yields: 2-4

20 shrimp, steamed with shell on
Soy Chili Sauce (recipe follows)

Need: steamer, pot or pan

Use shrimp of your choice. Steam until shrimp is well done. When ready to eat, peel each shrimp and dip into Soy Chili Sauce.

TIP: If you don't have a steamer, boil shrimp instead using a standardized pot or pan.

This is a good dish to eat while having a personal talk with friends or family, especially before or in between meals.

Soy Chili Sauce

This sauce can be used on just about
anything meaty like chicken and beef.

Prep time: 2 minutes
Yields: varies

1 - 2 Thai bird chili, sliced and de-seeded
3 tablespoons Bragg's Liquid Aminos
1 tablespoon green onion, sliced
½ teaspoon olive oil
½ teaspoon lemon juice

Need: pan

Prepare chili. Bring all ingredients together in a pan over medium heat. Simmer until bubbly. Remove from heat and pour a few spoonfuls over individual dipping bowls.

Napa Cabbage Roll

*Napa Cabbage Roll is a light and nutty treat
that may be cut into party squares.*

Prep time: 20 minutes
Cook time: 5 minutes
Yields: 2-3

¼ cup almonds
¼ cup cashews
¼ cup walnuts
¼ garlic clove
1 tablespoon Bragg's Liquid Aminos
9 ounces of medium soft tofu
6 Napa cabbage leaves
Soy Chili Sauce

Need: pan and food processor or blender

Coarse nuts, garlic, and Bragg's Liquid Aminos together in a food
processor or blender. Do not over blend. Set aside. In a pan, crumble
tofu in a pan and lightly heat. If preferred, use tofu straight from the
box. Blanch Napa cabbage in boiling water until soft, about 30
seconds to 1 minute. Remove cabbage, rinse in ice cold water and pat
dry. On a flat sturdy surface, cut out the Napa cabbage stem leaving
the soft leave. Line one Napa cabbage on a plate. Heap a spoonful of
nut mixture onto the cabbage. Top with crumbled tofu. Roll to close.
Dip with Soy Chili Sauce.

TIP: These wraps make an awesome main course dish. You will easily
be full on just two.

Stuffed Fuzzy Squash

The stuffing for this dish looks like it contains meat,
but it is a meat-free dish.

Prep time: 10 minutes
Cook time: 1 minute
Yields: 2-3 servings

1 fuzzy squash about 6 inches long
¼ cup almonds
¼ cup cashews
¼ cup walnuts
¼ cup pecans
1 really ripe green pear, chopped

Need: pot, food processor or blender, steamer

Puree all nuts until they are well chopped. Do not over puree and set aside. Wash and peel squash. Slice squash into 1 inch thick. Scoop out the middle where the seeds are. Be sure to not drill a hole through, leaving about ¼ inch thick on the bottom to hold the stuffing in. Steam squash until firm but not too soft. Add pear to nut. Scoop a spoonful onto the squash, covering the hole you made earlier.

TIP: Fuzzy melon or squash is found in most Asian supermarkets. You may also want to try using butternut, spaghetti, or your favorite squashes for this dish. If using a different squash, you can sprinkle the nut and pear mixture over the squash instead of stuffing it. You might also want to add a few spices like cinnamon and brown sugar to top it off.

Fish Ceviche over Fried Bean Curd

The salsa mixed with bean curd creates
a beautiful blend and balances flavor.

Fish Ceviche

Prep time: 15 minutes
Cook time: 30 minutes
Yields: 4 or more

1 cup of cooked fish (cod, sea bass, or tilapia)
¼ cup onion, minced
¼ cup tomatoes, finely chopped
2 Thai bird chili, diced and de-seeded
2 tablespoons of chopped jalapeno slices
1 teaspoon of olive oil
1 teaspoon of chopped cilantro
1 ½ teaspoon of Bragg's Liquid Aminos
Juice of one lime
A pinch of black pepper
1 block of bean curd, cut into ¼ inch thick squares
Oil for frying

Need: pan, grill, and deep fryer

Fish can be prepared any way you like it. Set the fish aside. In a bowl, add onions, tomatoes, chili, jalapeno, cilantro, and fish. Add lime, chili, olive oil, Bragg's Liquid Aminos, and black pepper. Let the salsa stand and chill in the refrigerator until ready to serve. Pan fry bean curd squares in oil, cover 1/3 of the bean curd until crispy and brown. You may also deep fry the bean curd in 365 degrees until they turn lightly brown. Spoon mixture onto bean curd.

The Other Chips & Dips

These fruit and vegetable chips go well with chili and black bean salsa.

Prep time: 20 minutes
Cook time: 15 minutes
Yields: 2-4

Enough plantain for your party
Enough taros for your party
Enough sweet potatoes for your party
Your favorite oil for frying
Suggested Dips

Need: deep fryer and peeler

Peel plantains, taro, and sweet potatoes. Cut plantains on the bias. Cut taros and sweet potatoes into thin rounds. Deep fry them until crispy and brown in 365 degrees heat. Transfer chips onto a plate lined with paper towel to drain off excess oil. Eat immediately as the chips will get soft.

TIP: If you don't have a deep fryer, pan fry them until the plantains, taros, and sweet potatoes are crispy, cooked, and browned.

SUGGESTED DIPS:

Turkey, beef, or vegetarian chili
Black bean and corn salsa

JAZZED UP BRUNCH

The weekends are sometimes full of surprises. It is a joyous time to celebrate life after an eventful week at work or at home if you are a stay at home mom. The weekend is the time to sleep in a tad bit later than usual, go on mini trips with the family, clean, or have brunch right in your own home. Like many restaurants that serve a brunch buffet, you can create your own Jazzed Up Brunch Buffet as well.

Now Serving...

Coconut & Nut Flat Cakes
Puffed Rice Cereal with Nuts & Fruits
Blueberry Surprise Fruit Ball
Creamy Rice Pudding
Seasoned Fruit Salad
Turkey Link & Patty
Sweet Potato Mash & Hash
Rice, Raisin, Nut Bar

Coconut & Nut Flat Cakes

This is almost like a pancake.

Prep time: 5 minutes
Cook time: 10 minutes
Yields: 2 rolls

½ cup gluten-free all purpose flour
½ cup unsweetened shredded coconut
¼ teaspoon salt
¼ teaspoon sugar or your favorite sweetener
1 cup coconut milk
½ cup of water
½ cup your choice of nuts chopped

Need: skillet, grill, or waffle maker

Combine flour, coconut, salt, sugar, coconut milk, water, and chopped nuts. Stir. Pour batter onto a hot skillet enough to cover the whole pan like making an omelet. Brown each side for about 1-2 minutes. This goes for using a grill. If using a waffle maker, cook until brown and crispy on the outside. Garnish with shredded coconut.

TIP: You can also add your favorite syrup or toppings to this. It doesn't hurt to try. Some suggested toppings include powdered sugar, pineapples, cinnamon, and honey.

Puffed Rice Cereal
with Nuts & Fruits

Your brunch isn't complete without cereal.

Prep time: 10 minutes
Yields: 1

¼ cup nut crumble (your favorite nuts chopped with cinnamon)
½ cup organic whole grain brown puffed rice
½ cup crispy brown rice cleaned milled and no sugar added
1 – 1 ½ cups almond or soy drink
Fruits like blueberries, raisins, strawberry, banana, kiwi

Need: blender or food processor

Chop nuts using a blender or food processor. Add cinnamon and set aside. Cut and chop up your favorite fruits. Add to cereal and serve with almond or soy drink.

TIP: In this recipe, you also have the flexibility to create a cereal to your liking. There are many types of nuts and fruits you can use. Now, there are also rice, oat, and hazelnut drink that can be used as a substitute for milk. Also, if you can't find crispy brown rice cereals, any type of rice crispy cereal will do. Always remember to read the labels.

Blueberry Surprise Fruit Ball

*A nutritious treat that can increase energy
in the morning or late afternoon.*

Prep time: 15 minutes
Cook time: 15 minutes
Chill time: 1 hour or overnight
Yields: Varies depending on size

1 cup dates, cooked
½ cup walnut
½ cup almond
½ cup pecan
1 cup raisins
½ cup un-sulphured dried cranberry
¼ cup blueberry
Toppings

Need: food processor or blender

Cook date in boiling water until soft for about 10 to 15 minutes. When cool, combine date, walnut, almond, pecan, raisins, and cranberry in a food processor and blend. Pulse until nuts are finely chopped and mixture is thick and sticky. When done, scoop a mixture and form into a round ball. Add one blueberry into the center and roll again until the fruit is hidden.

TIPS: If you want to add additional toppings to the outside, roll fruit ball into one or all of the following mixture and make sure to coat well, then chill or eaten right away. Again, you can play with the ingredients until you achieved desired results.

Toppings:

Ground or whole flaxseed
Shredded coconut
Toasted sesame seeds
Ground or whole sunflower seeds

Cream of Rice Pudding

This dish can almost pass as oatmeal. It has a light and nutty flavor.
Spice it up with cinnamon or raisins.

Prep time: 10 minutes
Cook time: 30-1 hour
Yields: 2-4

½ cup whole grain uncooked brown rice
2 ½ cups sweetened or unsweetened almond milk drink or soy
Optional Fruits, Nuts & Spice Toppings

Need: food processor and a small pot

Grind uncooked rice until reduced to ¼ of its original size. The smaller the rice pieces, the creamier pudding you will get and the faster it will cook. Wash rice several times and sieve through a colander. Pour rice into a pot and add almond or soy drink in medium heat. Bring to a boil, then simmer for about 20-30 minutes or longer, stirring frequently. Taste the pudding occasionally until you get the desired texture and consistency. Serve the way it is or add your favorite fruits, nuts or spices.

TIP: When the pudding cools, the rice thickens. It is best to eat pudding while hot. If you like your pudding to have more liquid, add more of the almond or soy milk. For creamier results, cook the rice longer and add more liquid to it.

Optional Fruit, Nut and Spice Toppings:

Raisins
Cranberries
Cinnamon
Banana
Maple syrup
Honey
Agave nectar
Fruit Preserves

Seasoned Fruit Salad

This fruit salad is simple and tropical. Can be eaten for breakfast,
lunch, or dinner. A great snack and a good pick-me-upper in the late
afternoon when energy level is low.

Prep time: 20-25 minutes
Yields: 2-4

½ cup of silken tofu, pureed
¼ cup of soy milk
A drizzle of your favorite sweetener
1 cup pineapple chunks
1 cup strawberries, halved
1 green Granny Smith apple, peeled and chopped
A pinch of salt
Juice of half a lime
Sliced almond pieces
Shredded coconut for garnish

Need: food process or blender

Puree tofu until smooth. Add your favorite sweetener, soy milk, and
set aside. In a bowl, add pineapples, strawberries, and apples. Lightly
season with salt, sweetener, lime juice, and toss. Drizzle tofu over
fruits. Top with toasted sliced almonds. Sprinkle some shredded
coconut over fruits for garnish.

Turkey Link & Patty

Try making your own link and patty with this dish.

Prep time: 15 minutes
Cook time: 15-20 minutes
Yields: 2

1 ½ cups ground turkey
¼ cup green onion, finely chopped
½ teaspoon white pepper
½ teaspoon ginger powder
1 tablespoon tapioca starch
A pinch of cayenne
Salt to and black pepper to taste

Need: deep fryer or pan

Mix everything together. Form into a link or patty. Pan fry until well done or until lightly crispy and brown. May deep fry at 365 degrees if desired.

Sweet Potato Mash & Hash

This is an alternative to hash browns.

Prep time: 2 minutes
Cook time: 20-30 minutes
Yields: 4

2 large sweet potatoes, cut into thin round slices
Oil for frying
Turkey bacon or nitrate and nitrite-free bacon (optional)

Need: pan, grill, or deep fryer

Boil peeled potatoes until almost cooked all the way. Cut potatoes into ¼ inch thick thin rounds and pan fry or deep fry them in 365 degrees until crispy. Transfer to a plate lined with paper towel to cool and drain off excess oil. Top with bacon bits. For an oil-free version, grill sweet potatoes and bacon until crispy.

Rice, Raisin, Nut Bar

This recipe was inspired by a lunch treat
I had during lunch in grade school.

Prep time: 1 minute
Yields: 1-2

1 cup raisins
1 cup peanuts or your choice of nuts
½ cup rice crispy

Need: food processor

In a food processor, process raisins and nuts until you reach a paste like consistency. Stir in rice crispy and form into a bar.

FIERY ENTREES

Classic Eastern and Western cuisines come together to create mouth watering savoring dishes. Sample the delights of Fiery Chicken Strips to Spinach Spaghetti in White Sauce. This section is divided into different categories, from Birds of a Flock, Meat Lover's Sensation, to Walking the Seafood Plank.

Now Serving...

BIRDS OF A FLOCK

Chicken Salad Spring Rolls
Stuffed Chicken with Creamed Spinach
Cornish Hen in Lime Pepper Sauce
Chilled Chicken Celery with Garlic Sesame Oil
Fiery Chicken Strips
Chicken & Ginger Stir-Fry
Quail with Scallion Lime Sauce

Chicken Salad Spring Rolls

If you like Vietnamese spring rolls, try this dish with chicken or tuna.

Prep time: 20-30 minutes
Cook: 15 minutes if using chicken
Yields: 2-4

1 pound boneless chicken breast, cooked and cubed
½ cup red onion, diced
½ cup celery, diced
2 tablespoons lime juice
¼ teaspoon salt
¼ teaspoon black pepper
1/8 teaspoon cayenne pepper
1/8 cup olive oil
A few sheets of rice or tapioca spring roll wrapper
A bunch of Romaine lettuce leaves, stem removed
½ cup cucumber, cut into long strips
Cilantro Lime Dipping Sauce

Need: large bowl and plate

In a large bowl, add chicken, red onion, celery, lime juice, salt, black pepper, cayenne pepper, and olive oil. Mix the chicken salad well and set aside. Get one sheet of spring roll wrapper and soften it by dipping it into a large bowl containing warm water for 2 seconds. Air dry onto a plate. When dry, lay a leaf of lettuce on the bottom. Lay a strip of peeled cucumber cut into thin strips lengthwise. Scoop chicken or tuna mixture onto the spring roll wrapper and fold like an egg roll. Dip into Cilantro Lime Dipping Sauce.

TIP: This recipe is good with tuna as well. If you use tuna, use 2 cans for two people and 4 for four people. If you use tapioca sheet, just note that it has a softer texture than rice wrapper.

Spring roll wrappers are found in Asian and some Latin markets.

Cilantro Lime Dipping Sauce

Prep time: 5 minutes
Yields: 2-4

2 teaspoons of cilantro, chopped
2 tablespoons of Bragg's Liquid Aminos
2 tablespoons lime juice
2 teaspoons olive oil
¼ teaspoon ground chili pepper
1 Thai bird and habanero chili pepper, chopped and de-seeded

Need: blender

If you like the sauce hot and spicy, add your favorite hot sauce. Otherwise, combine all ingredients in a blender and blend until smooth.

Stuffed Chicken with Creamed Spinach

Chicken and spinach make a good pair.

Prep time: 25 minutes
Cook time: 30-45 minutes
Yields: 4

2 cups spinach, chopped
2 cups watercress, chopped
1 garlic clove, finely chopped
3 ounces or ¼ cup of medium-firm tofu (optional)
¼ cup of olive oil
4 chicken breasts
½ cup organic apricot preserves
¼ cup ground flaxseed meal
Salt and white and black pepper to taste
Toothpicks

Need: food processor and oven

Chop spinach, watercress, garlic, tofu, and olive oil using a food processor. Blend until smooth and creamy. Season mixture with salt and pepper. Spread mixture over chicken breast. If the chicken breast is too thick, wrap it in saran wrap and pound with something hard to flatten breast before spreading mixture over chicken. Roll up and hold together with a sturdy toothpick. Season the outside of chicken with salt and white pepper. Evenly spread the apricot preserve onto the outside of the breast for a nice sweet and peachy flavor. Evenly coat the outside of chicken in flaxseed meal. Bake in 400 degrees for 30-45 minutes. It may take longer depending on size of chicken.

Cornish Hen in Lime Pepper Sauce

A favorite of mine for ages. So simple yet so tasty.

Prep time: 5 minutes
Cook time: 15-20 minutes
Yields: 2-4

1 cornish hen
½ teaspoon black pepper, eyeball it
½ teaspoon salt, eyeball it
Oil for frying
Lime and Black Pepper Sauce
Rice
Lettuce, tomato, cucumber, and onions as sides

Need: deep fryer or deep frying pot

Rub hen with salt and pepper inside and outside. Fry in a deep fryer for 10 minutes or longer at 365 degrees or until outside of skin is crispy and brown. If you don't have a deep fryer, cut the hen into fours and pan fry them in two inches of your favorite oil. Fry until brown on each side. When done, serve hen over a plate of rice, or over a bed of lettuce, tomato, cucumbers, and onion. Pour Lime and Black Pepper Sauce over hen.

Lime & Black Pepper Sauce

Prep time: 5 minutes
Yields: 4

½ cup lime juice
½ teaspoon black pepper
½ teaspoon salt

Need: a small container with lid

Combine all ingredients and shake well.

Chilled Chicken Celery with Garlic Sesame Oil

This dish turned me into a celery lover.

Prep time: 15 minutes
Cook time: 10 minutes
Chill time: one hour or overnight for better taste
Yields: 4

2 cups of cooked chicken drumsticks or thighs, shredded
A pinch of salt
3 celery stalks, cut into 3-inch length
5 garlic cloves, chopped
1 tablespoon olive oil
2 tablespoons sesame oil

Need: large pot

Leftover chicken from another night would be ideal to use for this dish. If not, prepare two cups of cooked shredded chicken. Season with salt.

In a pot, blanch celery in salt making sure not to overcook it. Remove celery, half it, and let cool in a separate bowl. In the same pot, brown garlic in olive oil. Add sesame oil. Drizzle part of the garlic sesame oil onto the celery and chicken. Coat well.

Line celery on the bottom of a large plate. If you have more celery than the plate can hold, stack the celery on top of each other. Next, completely cover celery with chicken. Add more chicken if needed. Pour more of the garlic sesame oil over chicken. Cover with a saran wrap and chill for about 2 hours. This dish is best served cold.

Fiery Chicken Strips

Just like how baked chicken should be.
You can't tell that no flour is used in this dish.

Prep time: 25 minutes
Stand: 2 hours +
Cook time: 30 minutes
Yields: 4

¼ - ½ cup olive oil
1 ½ garlic cloves
8 boneless chicken breast tenderloins
½ teaspoon cumin
½ teaspoon turmeric
½ teaspoon salt
½ teaspoon black pepper
1/8 teaspoon chili powder
Seasoned Dry Rub

Need: food processor or blender and oven

In a food processor, blend garlic and olive oil. Set aside. Season chicken with cumin, turmeric, salt, and pepper. Pour garlic oil onto the chicken and evenly coat. Let chicken marinade for two hours or longer.

In the mean time, work on the Seasoned Dry Rub. Dip each chicken strip into the dry rub and coat well.

Bake in 375 degrees for 25-30 minutes. For crispier and crunchy chicken, bake chicken at 400 degrees the last 5-7 minutes. Frequently check to make sure chicken is not overcooked.

Seasoned Dry Rub

Prep time: 5 minutes
Chill time: overnight
Yields: 3 cups

2 cups of fresh or canned garbanzo beans
1 cup crispy brown rice no sugar added (found in health food stores)
A pinch of salt
A pinch of black pepper

Need: food processor

If using fresh beans, prepare according to package directions. When done, grind the garbanzo beans and refrigerate overnight to dry. Do the same with canned garbanzo beans. Process all ingredients together using a food processor.

Chicken & Ginger Stir-Fry

Add a handful of ginger to this dish for a touch of spice.
This dish goes well with white basmati rice.
This dish is very soothing during Winter as it warms up the body.

Prep time: 15 minutes
Cook time: 20 minutes
Yields: 4

1 tablespoon of olive oil
2 cups of bone-in chicken, chopped
¼ cup chicken broth
1/8 cup Bragg's Liquid Aminos
¼ cup ginger, julienned
A pinch of sweetener
Black and white pepper to taste

Need: pot

Pour oil around outer edge of pot in medium to high heat. Add chicken and ginger until almost done before adding broth, sweetener, and Bragg's Liquid Aminos. Let broth evaporate. Once the chicken is done, serve over white jasmine or basmati rice.

Quail with Scallion Lime Sauce

An alternative to chicken dishes.

Prep time: 1 minute
Cook time: 20 minutes
Yields: 4

8 quails
¼ cup scallions, chopped
¼ cup of olive oil
A dash of salt and black pepper to taste
Scallion Oil (fried scallions in oil)
Lime & Black Pepper Sauce

Need: pan, oven, grill, or deep fryer

Quail can be prepared by baking, pan frying, grilled, or deep fried. The preferred choice is to deep fry quails in 365 degrees until quail is brown on the outside and cooked on the inside. When done, remove to a plate lined with paper towel. Brush Scallion Oil onto the quail. Dip quail into Lime & Black Pepper Sauce, a recipe found in this section.

Now Serving…

MEAT LOVER'S SENSATION

Beef Lettuce Wrap
Carrots & Daikon Slaw
Citrus Beef
Spicy Tofu in Meat Sauce
Tomato with Sweet Thai Basil

Beef Lettuce Wrap

This is a mini beef salad wrap in lettuce.

Prep time: 15 minutes
Stand time: 1 hour
Cook time: 15 minutes
Yields: 4

1 beef steak or sirloin enough for four
4 tablespoons Bragg's Liquid Aminos
½ teaspoon sweetener
1 teaspoon roasted sesame seed
¼ teaspoon sesame seed oil
1 tablespoon garlic, minced
½ teaspoon black pepper
2 tablespoons lime juice
1 bunch of Romaine lettuce

Need: indoor portable grill and large bowl

Combine all ingredients in a large bowl. Marinate beef for 1 hour. Grill beef and chopped into strips. Hold one Romaine lettuce in one hand. Add beef. Top with condiments or your favorite vegetables. Wrap to hold contents together.

TIP: This dish goes well with many fresh vegetables like carrots, cucumbers, and even red onions. Try with mints as well if you'd like.

Carrots & Daikon Slaw

This combination slaw goes well with spring rolls, marinated grilled beef, and in sauces that contain fish sauce.

Prep time: 5 minutes
Stand time: 15 minutes – 1 hour
Yields: 1 ½ cup

½ cup carrots, finely shredded
½ cup daikon, finely shredded
½ cup red onion, thinly sliced
½ cup raw apple cider vinegar or rice vinegar
1-2 tablespoons of sweetener of choice

Need: a container with lid

Combine carrots, daikon, red onion, vinegar, and sweetener. Let stand for 15 minutes or refrigerate longer until ready to use. The longer the slaw marinates, the better it tastes.

TIP: If you are using rice vinegar instead of raw apple cider vinegar, omit the sugar. The rice vinegar is sweet and is fine as is. If the vinegar is too strong for your taste, dilute it with ¼ - ½ cup of water.

If you like spicy, use a chili paste like Samba Oelek.

Citrus Beef

A good quality beef does make a difference in taste.
Choose a high quality beef like filet mignon.

Prep time: 5 minutes
Cook time: 10-15 minutes
Yields: 4

4 servings of good quality beef like filet mignon, cubed
2 tablespoons Bragg's Liquid Aminos
¼ cup orange juice
1-2 garlic cloves, minced
½ teaspoon of black pepper
1-2 tablespoons tomato sauce
1 tablespoon of olive oil
Fresh slices of tomatoes
Fresh slices of lettuce
Fresh slices of cucumber
Lime & Black Pepper Sauce

Need: wok or skillet

Marinade beef in Bragg's Liquid Aminos, orange juice, garlic, and pepper. Pan fry the beef in a wok or skillet using olive oil. Add the tomato sauce when beef is almost done. Serve over rice with tomatoes, cucumbers, and lettuce on the side. Pour Lime & Black Pepper Sauce over.

Spicy Tofu in Meat Sauce

The balance between the spiciness and flavors
make this dish go in perfect harmony.

Prep time: 5 minutes
Cook time: 15 minutes
Yields: 4

1 tablespoon of olive oil
1 garlic, minced
1 cup ground turkey or pork
½ teaspoon of salt
1 cup firm tofu, cut into thin slices
1-2 tablespoon of fermented black beans, lightly mashed
1 teaspoon of red chili pepper flakes
A dash of sweetener
A dash of black pepper
1 tablespoon of green onions, finely and thinly chopped

Need: skillet or wok

In a skillet or wok, add oil over medium heat. Swirl around before adding garlic. When garlic is lightly brown, add ground turkey or pork and salt. When meat is 90 percent done, add in tofu. Stir. Add fermented black beans, chili flakes, sweetener, and black pepper. Stir. Add in green onions. Stir. Remove from heat.

Tomato with Sweet Thai Basil

This is a sweet yet tangy dish. It goes well with rice.

Prep time: 10 minutes
Cook time: 15 minutes
Yields: 4

1 teaspoon of oil
1 garlic, minced
1 cup of ground turkey or ground pork
2 – 3 large tomatoes, cut into thin wedges
1/8 – ¼ cup of water or broth
1 tablespoon of basil, sliced into thin ribbons
Salt and black pepper to taste
A pinch of sweetener to taste

Need: wok or skillet

In a wok, add oil and garlic. Stir a few rounds. Add in meat. Stir until meat is done. Add tomatoes. Cook tomatoes until soft. Add water or broth and cover for a minute. Stir. Once the tomato softens and the meat is cooked, remove from heat. Stir in basil, salt, black pepper, and a dash of sugar. Add more sweetener if desired. Serve over rice or pasta.

TIP: The tomato is acidic and when eaten will be sour. Add sweetener until you achieve desired results.

Now Serving...

WALKING THE SEAFOOD PLANK

Cod in Roasted Red Pepper Sauce
Island Mahi Mahi with Pineapple Salsa
Crab Cakes
Kelp Salmon Roll
Garlic Lemon Peppered Shrimp
Tuna Black Bean Salad
Pan Fried Tilapia in Coconut Curry Sauce
Crispy Crunchy Salmon Cakes
Spicy Sardines in Tomato & Artichoke Sauce

Cod in Roasted Bell Pepper Sauce

Tired of tomatoes, have red pepper instead. Red pepper is loaded in nutrients and it packs up a punch as well.

Prep time: 20 minutes
Cook time: 20 minutes
Yields: 4

16 ounces of Cod fillet
A pinch of salt and pepper
¼ cup olive oil
½ cup red bell pepper
½ cup green bell pepper
½ cup yellow bell pepper
1 tablespoon of parsley
1/8 teaspoon cayenne
½ teaspoon salt
1 garlic clove

Need: skillet and food processor

Season cod fillet with salt and pepper. Pan fry in 2 tablespoons of olive oil until well done, about 2 minutes on each side, or until brown.

In a food processor, combine all three colored bell peppers, parsley, cayenne, salt, garlic, and olive oil. Pulse until ingredients are liquefied. Pour mixture over fish and simmer for about half a minute.

TIP: Another version is to transfer cooked fish to a plate and drizzle some of the Roasted Bell Pepper Sauce over the fish. Not cooking the vegetables prevents them from losing vitamins vital for our health.

Island Mahi Mahi with Pineapple Salsa

Let this dish sweep your mind to an island somewhere.
Think of the beauties of life and enjoy.

Prep time: 15 minutes
Marinade: 2 hours +
Cook time: 15 minutes
Yields: 4

16 ounces Mahi Mahi fillet
½ cup olive oil
3 tablespoon fresh oregano or 1 tablespoon dried
3 tablespoon fresh mint, chopped
2 garlic cloves, minced
¼ teaspoon basil, chopped
2 teaspoons lemon zest, julienned
½ cup lemon juice
¼ teaspoon salt and black pepper
Pineapple Salsa

Need: skillet and zip lock bag or large bowl

In a large zip lock bag or a bowl, marinate fish in the above ingredients for 2 hours or overnight. When you are ready to cook, pan fry fish until well done, which is when fish is flaky when picked with a fork. Top with pineapple salsa.

Pineapple Salsa

This side dish pairs well with plantains and refried or black beans.

Prep time: 10 minutes
Yields: 4

1 cup pineapple, chopped
½ cup grape tomatoes, halved
2 teaspoons olive oil
1-2 jalapeno chili, chopped and seeded
A pinch of salt and black pepper

Need: a bowl or container

Combine all ingredients together and mix well.

Crab Cakes

The fun thing about making crab cakes or any kind of seafood cakes is that you get to be creative and add anything you like.

Prep time: 30 minutes
Cook time: 30 minutes
Yields: 4

2 cups fresh crab meat, picked over or 2 canned of crab meat
1 cup fresh garbanzo beans or one 16 ounces canned of garbanzo bean
½ cup onion, chopped
2 garlic cloves
1½ tablespoons parsley
1½ tablespoons celery
¼ teaspoon ground coriander seed and cilantro
½ teaspoon cumin
¼ teaspoon baking powder (you can get one without aluminum and cornstarch)
1 cup of your oil for frying
Salt and pepper to taste
A pinch of cayenne pepper

Need: food processor and pan

In a food processor, combine beans, onion, garlic, parsley, celery, ground coriander seeds, cilantro, cumin, baking powder, and salt and pepper. Blend well until mixture reaches a thick paste-like consistency. Remove to a bowl. Add crab meat or fish. Stir until evenly coated. Scoop mixture and form into a patty. Place crab cakes onto a hot skillet in two inches of oil. Use less oil if desired. Fry until brown. You may deep fry it as well, which cooks faster and crab cakes come out crunchier.

Serve with your favorite dipping sauces. Plum sauce, hot sauce, and even some of the chili sauces found throughout this cookbook may be used.

TIP: For this dish, try exploring with various kinds of fish instead of crab.

Kelp Salmon Roll

An easy, mineral, and omega-3 rich dish.
Great as hors d' oeuvres or as an entrée.

Prep time: 20 minutes
Cook: 10 minutes
Yields: 4

2 sheets of dried kelp, soaked and softened
1-2 15 ounces canned pink salmon
¼ cup onion, minced
1 tablespoon toasted sesame seed
Juice from one lime
½ teaspoon black pepper
1 teaspoon tahini (optional)
¼ teaspoon cayenne pepper
2 pieces of Kimchi (optional)

Need: pan, large pot, plate, and bowl

To begin, cut two sheets of kelp and soak in cold water until soft, which is about 10-20 minutes. Once soft, blanch kelp in boiling water for 2 seconds, rinse in cold water, and let dry. If desired, add lemon to take out the sea taste.

Toast sesame seeds until light golden brown. Next, prepare filling. In a large bowl, combine salmon, onion, sesame seeds, lime juice, black pepper, tahini, and cayenne pepper. Mix until evenly coated.

Place a large sheet of kelp onto a flat sturdy surface or plate. Place ½ inch strip of Kimchi, only the Napa cabbage part, onto the kelp. Line a spoonful of the filling onto the large kelp going horizontally.

Roll twice so that the filling doesn't fall out. With a knife, cut where you stopped rolling. On the long roll, cut into four pieces.

Repeat until you run out of kelp and filling.

TIP: Kelp may be purchased at health food stores or at Asian supermarkets. They come dried in a package. Kimchi is a Korean mixture of vegetables fermented in chili sauce, which may be found in Korean supermarkets or selected Asian supermarkets.

Garlic Lemon Peppered Shrimp

Garlic and lemon always spice up a dish. This is one of them.

Prep time: 25 minutes
Cook time: 10 minutes
Yields: 4

1-2 cups shrimp, de-veined, and shelled
1 tablespoon olive oil
1 garlic, minced
1 shallot, minced
1 teaspoon black pepper
A pinch of salt
Juice of ½ lemon
A pinch of cayenne
1-2 Thai bird chilies for extra punch

Need: pot

Prepare shrimp. In a saucepan, add olive oil, garlic, shallot, black pepper, salt, lemon, chili, and cayenne. Stir for about a minute and add shrimp. Cook until shrimp is done.

Serve with a side of rice, avocado, and fresh steamed or grilled asparagus.

Tuna Black Bean Salad

Pack this dish with your favorite crackers or corn tortillas.

Prep time: 20-30 minutes
Chill time: 1 hour or overnight
Yields: 2-4

4 canned of tuna, drained
½ cup black olives, sliced
½ cup red onion, finely diced
½ cup tomatoes, finely diced
½ canned of black beans, drained and rinsed
½ canned of chickpeas, drained and rinsed
½ canned of corn kernels (optional)
Juice from half a lime
Season with salt and pepper

Need: a large container with lid

Combine all ingredients together and cover in the refrigerator until
ready to serve.

Pan Fried Tilapia
in Coconut Curry Sauce

*A friend and I made this dish together while I visited her in Miami.
It has a touch of Southeastern influence.*

Prep time: 20 minutes
Cook time: 25 minutes
Yields: 4

16 ounces tilapia fillet cut into squares
1 teaspoon of salt
1 teaspoon of black ground pepper
3 tablespoon of olive oil, coconut oil, or your favorite
¼ cup slivered almonds or crushed cashews, chopped (optional)
1 shallot, minced
1 garlic, minced
½ cup green bell pepper, diced
½ cup red bell pepper, diced
½ cup yellow bell pepper, diced
½ cup yellow crooked neck squash, diced
1 cup fresh coconut milk
¼ teaspoon cayenne pepper
1 tablespoon fresh cilantro, chopped
1 tablespoon fresh mint, chiffonade
1 tablespoon fresh basil, chiffonade

Need: skillet

Season tilapia with salt and black pepper. Set aside until ready to
cook. In a nonstick pan, pour one tablespoon of oil and turn heat
to medium-high. Stir in slivered almonds and let it toast before
adding in shallots and garlic. Next, add the green, red, yellow bell
peppers, and yellow squash. Reduce heat to low-medium. Stir

mixture until semi-cooked. Stir in the coconut milk. Add a pinch of salt and cayenne. Sprinkle mint, basil, and cilantro. Stir in fish. When done, remove from heat and plate up over a bed of rice or pasta.

Crispy Crunchy Salmon Cakes

Most seafood cakes are fried but try baking instead,
you get the crunch without the excess grease.

Prep time: 20 minutes
Cook time: 15 minutes
Yields: 2-4

14 ounces canned salmon or fresh salmon
½ cup onion, diced
1 tablespoon of green onions, chopped
¼ teaspoon ground ginger powder
1 ½ garlic, minced
1/8 teaspoon chili powder
5 tablespoon of ground chickpeas
Salmon Dry Rub

Need: oven and large bowl

In a large bowl, combine all ingredients together and mix well. Add about 5 tablespoons of ground chickpeas salmon to help hold the fish together. Form into a patty and coat each side well with the Salmon Dry Rub. Bake in the oven at 400 degrees for about 10-15 minutes until salmon cakes are golden brown.

Salmon Dry Rub

This rub can be used on chicken as well as beef.

Prep time: 5 minutes
Yields: 1 ½ cups

1 cup chickpeas
½ cup brown rice crispy, crushed
1 tablespoon ground milled flaxseed
A pinch of salt
A pinch of black pepper

Need: food processor

Grind chickpeas. Crushed rice crispy. In a bowl, combine, chickpeas, rice crispy, flaxseed, salt, and black pepper. Mix well.

Sardines in Spicy Tomato & Artichoke Sauce

*When you happen to have a can of sardines at home,
add marinated artichoke and eat it with rice crackers or gluten-free
toasted bread and you are set. Rice is good too.*

Prep time: 5 minutes
Cook time: 10 minutes
Yields: 1-2

1 canned sardines in tomato sauce
½ cup of marinated artichoke hearts already quartered
A few splashes of Bragg's Liquid Aminos
1 teaspoon of balsamic vinegar
½ teaspoon cayenne pepper
1 tablespoon jalapeno, diced

Need: skillet

In a skillet over medium heat, pour one canned of sardines. Chop the quartered artichokes in half. Add to sardines. Stir. Add in Bragg's Liquid Aminos, vinegar, cayenne, and jalapeno. When hot and bubbling, remove from heat.

TIP: Marinated jalapeno is best use with this dish, but fresh jalapeno is good too.

GRAIN LOVER'S PIZZAZ

There are many grains available today that give people more choices. There are grains such as rye, oats, corn, spelt, quinoa, and barley that serve as an alternative to wheat, but nonetheless, some of these grains contain gluten that people are sensitive too. Therefore, this cookbook focuses in on one grain only: rice. Whether it is a pasta, noodle, or plain rice dish, they are all rice based.

Even with these rice based dishes, you actually have control and freedom to substitute with other grains. Thanks to many products out there today, there are pastas made of corn, spelt, and quinoa. They come in many shapes and forms that you can create many combinations of dishes out of them. Although I zoom in on rice, you can zoom out to grains of your choice. That is the beauty of cooking. The freedom to choose and create.

Now Serving...

Rice Pasta with Sesame Beef
Spinach Spaghetti in White Sauce
Mac and Veggie Casserole
Chicken Tomato Sauce
No Wheat Noodle Thai Style
Glass Noodle Cabbage Wrap
Pineapple & Lentil Rice Surprise
Pineapple Fried Rice
Chickened Flavored Rice
Brown Rice Confetti
Rice & Potato Hash
Broccoli & Chicken Risotto

Rice Pasta with Sesame Beef

A Korean influenced dish using rice pasta and succulent beef.

Prep time: 20 minutes
Cook time: 30 minutes
Yields: 4

Sesame Beef Marinade (recipe follows)
1 package of brown rice pasta, found in specialty food stores
1 teaspoon roasted sesame seed
1 tablespoon olive oil
2 garlic cloves, minced
½ cup onion, julienned
¼ - ½ teaspoon sesame oil
½ teaspoon sweetener
½ cup fresh spinach
½ cup green onions, chopped on the bias
2 tablespoons Bragg's Liquid Aminos
A few sprigs of cilantro for garnish
Carrots and Daikon Slaw
Kimchi (optional)

Need: wok or frying pan and large pot

Marinate beef. Let stand. Prepare pasta according to package directions. Roast sesame seeds and set aside. In a wok or frying pan, add olive oil, marinated beef, garlic, onions, ¼ cup marinated Carrots and Daikon Slaw, the rest of the sesame oil, sweetener, and fry until beef is cooked and onions are soft. Add rice pasta, spinach, and green onions. Stir for about 1 minute and then stir in Bragg's Liquid Aminos. After evenly coated, remove from heat. Plate up and garnish with cilantro. Sprinkle with roasted sesame seeds. Top with some more of the Carrots and Daikon Slaw if desired.

TIP: Marinated Carrots and Daikon Slaw can be made ahead of time to expedite the process. It can be kept in the refrigerator for up to three days.

Sesame Beef Marinade

This dish is versatile and can be combined to make many dishes.

Prep time: 1 minute
Stand time: until ready to cook with it

4 ounces of beef sirloin, 1 ounce per person
1 tablespoon Bragg's Liquid Aminos
1/8 teaspoon of sesame oil

Need: wok or frying pan

Combine ingredients together and mix well. Let stand covered while you work on the pasta.

TIP: This dish can be prepared in numerous ways. It does not have to be used solely for the Rice Pasta with Sesame Beef dish. Sesame Beef Marinade can be skewered and grilled. It can serve as a substitute for other beef dishes. It can even be cooked with broccoli to make Broccoli and Beef.

The fun part is what you make out of it. The key is you. You are in control.

Spinach Spaghetti in White Sauce

There is no milk and cheese in this recipe, but the sauce is scrumptiously delicious and is very easy to make. I received raves on this dish.

Prep time: 25 minutes
Cook time: 25 minutes
Yields: 3-4

6 ounces or more of spinach rice pasta
1 cup frozen spinach
5 garlic cloves, minced
5 shallots, minced
2/3 cup shrimp with head on, shelled and de-veined
9 ounces medium soft tofu
¼ - ½ cup chicken broth
1 tablespoon extra virgin olive oil

Need: blender, large pot and saucepan

Prepare pasta according to package directions. While pasta cooks, puree tofu and broth together in blender. Puree until you get a smooth and thick texture. Set aside. In a saucepan, add oil, garlic, and shallot. Stir for about a minute in medium to high heat to get the garlic and flavor out. Be sure not to overcook the garlic as it browns easily. Next, add spinach and shrimp with head on. Stir until shrimp is done. Stir in pasta. Voila!

TIP: When pureeing tofu, use less broth if you prefer a very creamy sauce. For the shrimp, you can leave a few shrimp with head on to give the sauce more flavors. Too much can be overpowering.

Mac & Veggie Casserole

Instead of mac and cheese, this is mac and veggie.

Prep time: 25 minutes
Cook time: 15 minutes
Yields: 4-6

2 medium Yukon Gold Potatoes, diced
3 carrots, diced
1/8 bag of frozen peas
¼ cup brown rice elbow macaroni
2 cups chicken, cooked and shredded
12 ounces soft tofu
5 shitake mushrooms, soaked and sliced
¼ cup chicken broth
1/8 in ginger
1½ garlic clove
1-2 Serrano chilies
½ of a medium onion, minced
1 teaspoon of olive oil
½ - 1 teaspoon of fine salt
1 cup of yellow squash, diced or shredded (optional)

Need: several pots and pans, oven and food processor

Boil potatoes, carrots, and peas together or in separate pot until almost fully cooked. Drain and set aside. Cook macaroni according to package directions. Next, puree together ginger, garlic, chilies, and 1 tablespoon of broth. Set aside. In a skillet, add olive oil over medium heat. Add onions, the pureed mixture, shitake mushrooms and stir for about 30 seconds to 1 minute to bring out the mushroom flavor. While that cooks, puree tofu in ¼ cup of broth and add mixture to mushrooms. Stir. Add in chicken, macaroni, peas, carrots, and potatoes to the creamed mixture. Add salt. Stir well and pour onto a baking dish. Top with yellow squash. Cover and bake for 15 minutes in 365 degrees. Remove foil during the last five minutes. Let the casserole sit in the oven for an additional 5 minutes before removing from oven.

No Wheat Noodle Thai Style

This dish is almost similar to a dish called Pad Thai.

Prep time: 15 minutes
Cook time: 25 minutes
Yields: 3

Spicy Cashew Tamarind Sauce (recipe follows)
6 ounces package of brown rice spaghetti or rice fettucine
½ -1 cup chicken breast, thinly sliced
½ - 1 cup shrimp, shelled and de-veined
1 cup of bean sprouts, washed
¼ teaspoon sweet Thai basil, cut into ribbons
1 tablespoon olive oil
Cilantro for garnish
Basil for garnish
Cashews, chopped (optional)

Need: skillet or wok

Prepare Spicy Cashew Tamarind Sauce and set aside. Cook pasta according to package directions. In a skillet, add oil, half of the garlic and shallots. Stir and cook until soft and lightly brown. Stir in chicken and about a tablespoon of broth. When chicken is almost done, add in shrimp and bean sprouts. Stir before adding in the pasta. Stir. Add in Spicy Cashew Tamarind Sauce and stir until noodles are evenly coated. Plate up and eat. Garnish with cilantro, basil, and cashews.

TIP: If you want to break away from eating rice, try this dish with yellow squash. Use a spiral slicer to shred squash.

Spicy Cashew Tamarind Sauce

A touch of spice enlivens a dish.
You can kick up a few notches by adding more chili.

Prep time: 10 minutes

3 tablespoons fish sauce
3 tablespoons tamarind sauce
3 tablespoons Bragg's Liquid Aminos
¼ cup chicken broth
Juice from ½ a lime
1 teaspoon ginger or dry ginger powder
1 teaspoon galangal
1 garlic, minced
1 shallot, minced
1-2 Thai bird chili, sliced and de-seeded

Need: blender and small container with lid

Combine fish sauce, tamarind sauce, Bragg's Liquid Aminos, broth, lime juice, ginger, galangal, garlic, shallots, and chili. Blend well and pour to a small container.

TIP: The tamarind is best mixed with 3 tablespoons of water to soften.

Glass Noodle Cabbage Wrap

You can wrap anything you like with this dish.

Prep time: 15 minutes
Cook time: 15 – 30 minutes
Yields: 4

1 bundle of bean vermicelli or glass noodle
8 cabbage leaves
½ teaspoon of olive oil
1/8 teaspoon fresh ginger, finely chopped
2/3 cup ground turkey
A pinch of salt
2 tablespoon green onions, chopped
1/8 teaspoon cilantro, chopped
2 tablespoon Bragg's Liquid Aminos
1/8 – ¼ teaspoon white pepper
1 teaspoon toasted black sesame seeds

Need: pots

Cook vermicelli or glass noodle according to package directions. Once soft, immediately remove from heat and drain. Set aside to dry. If using glass noodle, cut into smaller pieces, about 3 inches in length.

In another pot, blanch cabbage leaves with stem removed, in boiling water for 30 seconds or until soft. Remove and submerge into ice cold water and let dry on paper towel.

In a skillet, add olive oil, ginger, salt, and turkey. Stir until turkey is done. Add noodle, green onions, cilantro, Bragg's Liquid Aminos, and white pepper. Stir until evenly coated. Add black sesame seeds. Stir before removing from heat. Scoop a mixture onto the cabbage leaves and roll.

Serve with your favorite dipping sauce or the sauces found throughout this cookbook.

TIP: An alternative version to this is to bake the stuffed cabbage in the oven at 350 degrees for 15-30 minutes, or until cabbage becomes supple and brown. The brown color gives cabbage a toasty and nutty flavor.

Pineapple & Lentil Rice Surprise

With this dish, you get fruit, vegetables, grain, and protein in one meal.

Prep time: 10 minutes
Cook time: 1 hour
Yields: 4

2 cups cooked brown rice
2 cups cooked green lentils
1 ½ cup fresh pineapple, chopped
½ cup tomatoes, chopped
½ cup onions, diced
1/8 teaspoon cayenne pepper
A pinch of salt and pepper
1 tablespoon Bragg's Liquid Aminos
2 teaspoons of fish sauce (optional)
1 teaspoon of tamarind sauce (optional)
2 tablespoons of pineapple juice

Need: rice cooker, pot and large bowl

Cook lentils according to package directions until tender but not too soft, which is about one hour. While lentils cook, chop pineapples into bite size pieces. Prepare tomatoes and onion. In a large bowl, add pineapple, tomatoes, onions, cayenne, salt, pepper, Bragg's Liquid Aminos, fish sauce, tamarind sauce, and pineapple juice. Stir and set aside. Add rice and lentils when done. Mix well. Chill and serve.

TIP: Rice may be cooked over stove top. Follow package directions if using this option. If preparing rice using a rice cooker, use 2 to 2 ½ and a half cups of water per 1 cup of rice.

Pineapple Fried Rice

It is hard to picture eating fruits with rice, but not with this dish.
The flavors balance each other out nicely.

Prep time: 20 minutes
Cook time: 20 minutes
Yields: 2-3

15 shrimp, shelled and de-veined
A pinch of salt
1 ½ cooked brown rice
½ cups pineapple chunks
¼ teaspoon ginger powder
¼ teaspoon garlic powder
¼ teaspoon white pepper
1 teaspoon fish sauce
1 teaspoon Bragg's Liquid Aminos
1 tablespoon green onion, thinly sliced
1 teaspoon basil
½ tablespoon olive oil
1-2 Thai bird chili peppers

Need: wok or pan

Add olive oil to wok. When oil starts to sizzle, cook shrimp and season with a pinch of salt. Stir in rice, add pineapples, ginger and garlic powder, and white pepper. Stir well. Stir in fish sauce and Bragg's Liquid Aminos. Stir again. Add in green onions, basil, and chili peppers. Remove from heat and plate up.

Chicken Flavored Rice

1 cup white basmati rice
2 cups chicken broth

Need: rice cooker

Wash rice several times to remove excess starch. Put rice in rice cooker and add chicken broth.

Brown Rice Confetti

*This seemingly bland dish of rice explodes in colors and flavors
with an added touch of beans and vegetables.*

Prep time: 5 minutes
Cook time: 20-25 minutes
Yields: 4

4 servings of cooked brown rice
½ teaspoon of olive oil
½ cup of corn kernels, drained and rinsed
½ cup of red bell pepper, diced
½ cup of black beans
Season with salt and pepper
A few splashes of lime juice (optional)

Need: rice cooker or pot

In a large bowl, add rice. Drizzle rice with olive oil, corn, bell pepper,
black beans, salt, pepper, and lime juice if desired.

Rice & Potato Hash

This dish does away with the ordinary plain rice.

Prep time: 5 minutes
Cook time: 10 minutes
Yields: 2

2/3 cup cooked brown rice
½ cup cooked red potatoes, semi-mashed
1/8 cup red bell pepper, minced
1/8 cup green bell pepper, minced
1/8 cup yellow bell pepper, minced
1 teaspoon onion, finely chopped
1 teaspoon green onion, finely chopped
A pinch of garlic powder
A pinch of salt
A pinch of white pepper

Need: skillet, indoor portable grill or deep fryer

In a large mixing bowl, combine rice and potatoes. Mash together until you get a thick patty like consistency. Add the remainder of the ingredients. Mix well. Scoop ¼ of the mixture or more onto your hand and form into a patty. Deep fry or pan fry until rice and potato patties are crispy or light golden brown. Serve with steamed vegetables of choice like cauliflower or broccoli.

TIP: This dish is very aromatic when rice is crispy. To make it crispy, add more oil. Grilling it is another option. It requires less oil.

Broccoli & Chicken Risotto

Chicken, broccoli, rice, and more.
You get a nice serving of vegetables with this dish.

Prep time: 15 minutes
Cook time: 25 minutes
Yields: 2-3

½ teaspoon olive oil
¼ cup cooked chicken, shredded
¼ cup onion, diced
¼ cup red bell pepper, diced
¼ cup broccoli, diced
¼ cup edamame pods, shelled
¾ cup Arborio rice
½ cup broth
1 cup of water
¼ teaspoon turmeric powder
¼ teaspoon ginger powder
A pinch of salt and black pepper to taste
A pinch of white pepper

Need: pot or rice cooker

Add oil to a pot over medium heat. Add chicken, onions and stir several times before adding in red bell pepper, broccoli, and edamame pods. Stir a few times before adding in the rice. Stir until evenly coated. Add broth. Stir again. Transfer to a rice cooker. Add water, turmeric, ginger powder, and salt, and black and white pepper. Stir rice well. When rice is done, let it sit in the rice cooker for about 5 to 10 minutes to dry. Serve with beef skewers or any of your favorite side dishes.

TIP: Risotto is usually prepared over stove top and rice usually cooks in about 20 minutes. However, I use a rice cooker because it is more convenient for me.

DESSERT PARADISE

A mentor once sent me an e-mail about the importance of eating dessert first. What she meant is that sometimes, when we are very busy with life, we forget to live in the present. When we have a bite of sweet tasting piece of dessert, it awakens, soothes and comforts us. Our worries disappear. We forget about everything else except eating and savoring every bite of that piece of cake, ice cream, or cookies, in our mouth. Therefore, this cookbook is not complete without desserts and drinks.

The desserts in this cookbook are not unusual, but they are different from what I and many are used to. The ingredients use are vegetables, fruits, nuts, rice, and even tea that paint a palate of desserts in this section, I call a Dessert Paradise. In some extent, the flavors of some dessert like Cinnamon Fried Plantains and Young Coconut with Water Chestnut Juice, take me, at times, to paradise. It is usually the flavors that have that effect on our senses. Remember, eat your dessert first!

Now Serving...

Tofu Raspberry & Blueberry Parfait with Nut Crumble
Tofu Flower with Ginger Essence
Green Tea Gelatin
Fried Taro in Jujube Sauce
Cinnamon Fried Plantains with Rice Ice Cream
Banana Pudding
Black Rice in Coconut Cream
Purple Passion
Purple Yam Delight with Toasted Coconut
Sesame Crunch
Flat Macaroons
Plum & Date Ale
Golden Raisin Ice
Tropical Fruit Delight
Young Coconut & Water Chestnut Juice
Papaya Smoothie
Raspberry Dream

Tofu Raspberry & Blueberry Parfait with Nut Crumble

A red, white, and blue sensation.

Prep time: 15 minutes
Cook time: 15 minutes
Yields: 4

1 box or 16 ounces silken tofu
½ cup fresh raspberries
½ cup fresh blueberries
½ cup of your favorite nuts, chopped
A dash of cinnamon
¼ cup water
6 slices of fresh ginger root
½ cup water
½ cup sweetener

Need: food processor and saucepan

In a food processor, chop nuts. Add a dash of cinnamon. Set aside. Prepare ginger syrup by combining ginger, water, and sweetener and bring to a boil. Lower heat to low and simmer syrup for about 5 minutes. Remove syrup from heat. In a cup, cut tofu about ½ inches thick to fit inside the bottom of a cup or plate. Pour a spoonful of the ginger syrup over the tofu. Add fresh berries and some of the nut crumble mixture. Repeat for another two layer depending on how deep your cup or plate is. Top with some more of the nut mixture.

TIP: For a stronger ginger flavor, simmer the syrup longer and sweetener during this process. Condense the syrup a bit.

Tofu Flower with Ginger Essence

This dessert is similar to the tofu parfait recipe except this warm delight is best eaten hot. It is very comforting after breakfast during the winter before you start the day as it warms up the stomach and gives you the energy you need for a days worth of hard work.

Prep time: 10 minutes
Cook time: 15 minutes
Yields: 1-4

1-2 boxes of silken tofu
1 cup of water
10 slices of ginger
Sweetener of choice

Need: steamer or microwave

In a steam safe bowl, steam the tofu until hot. Time usually varies depending on the size of the steamer. Liquid will come out from the bowl of tofu, which is good. You don't want to throw this reserve away. Prepare the ginger syrup by adding water, slices of ginger, and sweetener. Bring to a boil and simmer until syrup is condensed. Pour syrup over tofu and serve immediately while hot.

TIP: If you don't want to waste the ginger, blend a cup of water in the ten slices of ginger. Add more ginger if you like. You can sieve the ginger after you blend it to remove excess pulp. If you like it with pulp, that's fine. Pour the puree ginger into a pot and add agave nectar. A quicker version to prepare this syrup is to blend the ginger in water. Bring to a boil. Remove from heat and then add the agave nectar

Green Tea Gelatin

Definitely something to try, not just with green tea, but jasmine and black, and maybe even your favorite fruits.

Prep time: 10 minutes
Cook time: 1 minute
Chill time: 30 minutes - 1 hour
Yields: 2-4

2 teaspoons of agar agar powder
1-3 packs of green tea powder
2 cups of water
1-2 teaspoons of sweetener

Need: your favorite gelatin mold and a pot

Per one cup of liquid, add two teaspoons of agar agar powder. Bring to a boil and pour to a mold. Add more agar agar if you want gelatin to be firm. If you prefer the gelatin to be softer, add less of the agar powder.

Green tea gelatin: In a saucepan, brew one cup of green tea along with two teaspoons of agar agar powder and sweetener. Bring to a boil and pour to a mold. Chill.

TIP: Try this dessert with other teas, soy milk, and coconut milk. Agar agar gels and thickens quickly. You can have your dessert in less than an hour depending on the size and amount of gelatin you make.

Fried Taro in Jujube Sauce

Frying this vegetable turns this dish into a dessert.

Prep time: 10 minutes
Cook time: 15 minutes
Yields: 2-4

6 small taros, sliced
¾ cup white rice flour
¼ cup brown rice flour
1/8 cup tapioca starch
2 tablespoons sweetener
½ teaspoon salt
1 ¼ cups coconut milk
½ cup jujube dates
1/8 cup water
Frying oil of choice
Sprinkle of sweetener

Need: deep fryer and food processor

Cook the dried red date in water until soft. While that cooks, peel the taro and cut into large chunks. Prepare taro batter by combining all dry ingredients together before adding the liquid mixture. Dip taro slices in the batter. Deep fry taro in 365 degrees until cooked and lightly brown. Transfer taro to a paper toweled plate to cool and drain off excess oil. When the date is soft, remove pit if any. Puree the date with the water until you get a smooth consistency and set aside. Pour date sauce over fried taro. Lightly sprinkle or drizzle your favorite sweetener. Chill in the refrigerator for about 1 hr.

Cinnamon Fried Plantains
with Rice Ice Cream

A crunchy and fruity dessert, an alternative to potato chips.

Prep time: 10 minutes
Cook time: 20 minutes
Yields: 2-3

1 plantain banana
¾ cup white rice flour
¼ cup brown rice flour
1/8 cup tapioca starch
2 tablespoons of sweetener
½ teaspoon salt
½ cup unsweetened shredded coconut
1 ¼ cup coconut milk
Frying oil
A dash of cinnamon
1 ½ toasted white and black sesame seeds
A tub of rice ice cream

Need: deep fryer or a pot

Cut plantains on the bias. In a separate bowl, combine all dry ingredients. Add coconut milk and sweetener and stir well. Deep fry in 365 degrees or pan fry in two inches of oil until brown and crispy. Remove and let cool onto a plate lined with paper towel. Sprinkle cinnamon and drizzle more sweetener on to the plantain. Serve with two scoops of rice ice cream.

NOTE: This dish can be eaten as a side dish or as a dessert.

Banana Pudding

Prep time: 5 minutes
Yields: 2

½ cup silken tofu
1 large frozen banana
½ cup soy or almond milk
Toasted sliced almonds

Need: blender

Blend. Serve immediately.

Black Rice in Coconut Cream

This is a very aromatic dessert.
Using fresh coconut juice or milk is the key to this recipe.

Prep time: 10 minutes
Cook time: 30 minutes
Yields: 2-4

½ cup black rice
1½ cups water
1 teaspoon sweet rice flour or tapioca starch
1 canned of 16 ounces organic coconut milk
Sweetener
Salt

Need: rice cooker and pot

Pre-wash rice. Soak in water for about 5 minutes. Drain and cook rice in 1½ cups of fresh water or you can use the same water used to soak the rice. Add salt and tapioca starch. While the rice cooks, work on the coconut cream. In a separate pot, bring coconut milk and sugar to a boil. Top rice with as much coconut cream as you'd like.

Purple Passion

Let this purple passion sweep you off your feet.
A light and aromatic treat.

Prep time: 20 minutes
Cook time: 30 minutes
Yields: 4

½ cup purple yam, diced
½ cup cassava or yucca, diced
½ cup baby taro, diced
3 tablespoons of tapioca pearl
½ cup multicolored tapioca shreds
5 cups of water
1 cup coconut milk
Sweetener

Need: pot and steamer

The quickest way to prepare this dessert is to steam the yam, yucca, and taro together until they are all soft. While you do that, prepare a pot full of coconut milk, water, and tapioca and tapioca shreds that have been soaked. Cook until tapioca is translucent and not white and the tapioca shreds are soft. When done, remove from heat. When the yam, yucca, and taro are done, dice them and add to the coconut milk. Stir and bring to a boil.

Although this version is the quickest and easiest way, it might not bring out the flavor you should aim for.

The other version, which requires more strength to cut and dice the raw yam, yucca, and taro because these vegetables are very tough and fibrous, it is well worth the effort though. When the dessert is done, it will bring out a nice flavor.

For this version, you want to peel the yam, yucca, and taro. Dice and cook it together with the coconut milk like the first version. You will have to cook it until the yam, yucca, and taro are soft. Cook until done in low to medium heat stirring frequently.

Purple Yam Delight
with Toasted Coconut

Love the color in this dessert.

Prep time: 1 minute
Cook time: 25 minutes
Yields: 1

1 purple yam
¼ cup toasted coconut

Need: steamer, food processor and skillet

Steam yam until soft. Puree yam in a blender or food processor. Top with toasted coconut.

Sesame Crunch

Sesame peanut crunch was a snack enjoyed by the elderly while growing up. I can see why they like it.

Prep time: 10 minutes
Yields: 2-4

1 cup raisins
½ cup peanuts or cashews
½ cup toasted sesame seeds

Need: food processor

Toast sesame seeds. Process raisins and peanuts or cashews together. In a loaf pan, press mixture evenly onto the pan. Cut into a few rectangular bars. Dip into sesame seeds. Eat right away or chill.

Flat Macaroons

A very coco-nutty treat.

Prep time: 5 minutes
Cook time: 15
Yields: 1-2

½ cup shredded coconut
1 cup coconut milk
1 tablespoon agave nectar
¼ cup brown rice flour
1/8 cup tapioca starch
¼ teaspoon salt

Need: skillet and indoor portable grill

Combine dry ingredients together. Combine liquid. Mix both together. Pan fry first on a skillet then transfer to a grill. Flat Macaroons are done when the outside is lightly brown and crispy.

Plum & Date Ale

An ale to toast with any dish.

Prep time: 2 minutes
Cook time: 15 minutes
Yields: 1

2 teaspoons fresh umeboshi plum paste
½ cup red dates, cooked and pitted
1 cup sparkling water, mineral water, or club soda
1 sprig of mint

Need: food processor

In a food processor, blend plum paste and cooked soft dates. Remember to remove pit. Pour mixture into a glass. Add water. Top with a sprig of mint.

Golden Raisin Ice

This golden raisin ice is a light and refreshing treat.

Prep time: 5 minutes
Cook time: 15 minutes
Yields: 4

1 cup golden raisins
4 cups water
Ice
Sweetener

Need: blender and pot

In a deep pot, add water and raisins. Bring golden raisins to a boil. Simmer for about 5-10 minutes to let the raisins release their flavor. Scoop about ¼ of the raisins, ½ cup of the raisin syrup, and chunks of ice onto a blender. Blend raisins, ice, raisin syrup, and sweetener. Drink immediately.

A quick version to this is instead of blending is to scoop a mixture of the raisins and a cup or two cups of the raisin syrup onto a tall glass. Add ice.

Tropical Fruit Delight

As the name suggests, this is certainly tropical, fruity, and delightful.

Prep time: 15 minutes
Cook time: 10-15 minutes
Yields: 1

32 ounces of fresh coconut milk
1 teaspoon of small tapioca pearl
½ cup fresh fruits, chopped to small pieces
Sweetener
Ice

Need: pot and tall glass

Fruits to use:

Jackfruit
Longan
Lychee
Rumbatan
Pineapple
Kiwi
Star fruit
Honeydew melon
Watermelon

Soak the tapioca in water for about 5 minutes. Cook tapioca in coconut milk until tapioca is translucent and expand in size. At this point, remove from heat. When cooled, add fruits. If the coconut is too strong, dilute with water, but the stronger the taste, the better. Add sweetener and ice and pour to a tall glass.

Young Coconut & Water Chestnut Juice

Prep time: 20 minutes
Yields: 1

1 young coconut
¼ cup chopped fresh water chestnuts

Need: coconut cracker and tall glass

Chill the coconut ahead of time before use. Chilling the young coconut gives it a very refreshing taste. Crack open the young coconut. Strain the juice onto a glass and scoop the young coconut meat and add to the juice. Add ¼ cup of fresh water chestnuts into the glass. Serve chilled.

Papaya Smoothie

*Papaya is healthy and good for the skin
and has enzymes that help the digestive system.*

Prep time: 15 minutes
Yields: 1

1/2 cup unsweetened or sweetened almond, soy, or rice drink
1 cup fresh papaya
A drizzle of sweetener

Need: blender

Combine everything into a blender. Drizzle with your favorite sweetener.

Raspberry Dream

*Raspberries are good for us not only because of it is bright red color but,
it is awesome because it is low in sugar too.*

1 cup frozen raspberries
1 cup apple juice
1 tablespoon tofu

Need: blender

Blend. Serve immediately.

TIPS FOR MODERN DAY
LIVING AND EATING

At this point, you have sampled what it takes to start a new culinary experience. I hope you will continue on this journey for a life time of good eats. This last part of the book will equip you with tips and resources to guide you on your journey.

When we eat foods that taste good, our body is happy and we feel it too. It is as if we have suddenly become alive and awakened. Do you remember an occasion where you were happy after eating a meal? Your mood was up and everything just seemed to go well? That is what eating should be, pleasant and enjoyable. Often, in our time-pressured society, we forget that the simple things in life can make a huge difference in how we feel. We might not feel or notice the minute changes at first, but keep it up and you will reap in the rewards.

Chewing food meticulously. *Swallowing food without chewing it well makes it harder for your body to digest and requires it to expend more energy. In living in the present moment, there is time. There is time to enjoy. This means we have the time to eat and chew well.*

Enjoying what we eat. *How often do we eat for pleasure and enjoyment? A lot of times, we eat because we are hungry. We eat because* we have to. We eat because we are bored or faced with a problem from which we want to escape. Sometimes, we eat because it is programmed into our minds to eat three times a day. Eating has become a routine. We forget to enjoy our meals and savor each bite.

Everything is good for us. *Enjoy what Nature has provided for us. Appreciate the foods that we have. Now, a word of caution. If you are allergic to some foods, do not eat it, and definitely follow your medical doctor's advice.*

Eat everything in moderation. *Too much of one thing is not good, and too little is not good either. Moderation is key.*

Break the cycle. *Eat a variety of foods and try new things. This gives time for the body to remove toxins.*

Establish a relationship with the foods you consume. *Make peace with the food you consume even if you happen to eat something you know you are not supposed to.*

Find the right fit for you. *There is no one right plan or one wrong plan. Each person is unique, and circumstances are different. What one needs is a plan that works for him or her and not merely sticking to a plan because it helps someone else and you believe it will help you too. Choose one that fits you best and be sure to modify it to fit your lifestyle.*

Think harmony and balance.

Eat frequently and in smaller portions. *In college, my professor told us that eating should be done frequently. Listen to your body.*

Reprogram old eating beliefs. *Replace thoughts with positive affirmations about eating.*

Next time when you prepare your meals, remember to follow these simple steps. Although they are principles you already know, they are an invaluable tool to have. Knowledge is power and knowledge is only half the battle. The other half is knowing what to do with the knowledge. It is applying it in your daily life.

PART III: RESOURCES

The following list of resources is meant as a guide only. It is important to remember that a therapy that may work for one individual may not work for majority since we are all different. Research on your own to see if that particular resource is of benefit to you.

Whenever you begin something, consult your medical doctor before exploring any alternative treatment. The list provided is for your information only and does not make any claims or guarantees or cure a particular disease.

Therapies that may help:

NAET (Nambudripad's Allergy Elimination Technique)
EFT (Emotional Freedom Technique)
Biofeedback
Acupuncture
Acupressure
Body work
Bowen Therapy
Ayurveda
Reflexology
Massage Therapy like Shiatsu
Reiki
Nutri-Energetics System

Various Diet Therapies that may help improve health and healing process:

Macrobiotic
Raw food
Blood type
Metabolic
Vegetarian
No carbohydrates

Books that can help enlighten you emotionally, physically, and spiritually:

Food as Medicine by Dr. Dharma Singh Kalsa
The Allergy and Asthma Cure by Dr. Fred Pescatore
Nutrition and Physical Degeneration by Weston Andrew Price

Certified Natural Health Practitioners and Food Coach:

In-Joy Nutrition and Body Works
Contact: Brenda Brisco, CNHP, RMT
E-mail: briscoeb@in-joy.us

La Bella Body
Contact: Hayley Hines, Healthy Living Coach/Chef, and Registered Yoga and Massage Therapist
E-mail: Hayley@labellabody.com

Where to buy and shop:

www.sprouts.com
www.wholefoods.com
www.wildoats.com

www.cupboardnaturalfoods.com
www.traderjoes.com
www.organicconsumers.org
www.tinkyada.com

Regardless of where you are, you can find health food stores by going online to Organic Consumers. They have a section where you can find stores listed in your area.

Printed in the United Kingdom by
Lightning Source UK Ltd., Milton Keynes
137012UK00001B/74/A